I Always Win!

Written by
Rob Waring and **Maurice Jamall**

Before You Read

to remember

a race

to win

starting line

corner

trees

cup

fast

finish line

gate

second, first, third

In the story

Tyler

Ryan

Mr. Walsh

"Are you ready, Tyler?" asks his friend, Eric.
"Yes, I'm ready," Tyler replies.
Today is a big day in Bayview. There is a big bike race today. Everybody is very excited. Ryan is in the race, too. Tyler and Ryan are both very good riders. They both want to win the race.

Tyler's friends John, and Eric want him to win.
"Have a good race, Tyler," says Eric.
"Thanks, I want to win this year," says Tyler.
John says, "Ryan wins every year. But I think you'll win today."
"Be careful of Ryan. He's very fast," says Eric.
"I know," Tyler replies. "I'll watch him."

Ryan is with his father, Mr. Walsh. Ryan has a new bike. Every year Ryan's father buys him a new bike for this race. It is a very good bike. It is very fast. Ryan is very happy. "I'll win this race again this year, too, with my new bike," Ryan thinks.

Ryan's father is talking to Ryan.
"I want you to win. Our family always finishes first,"
Mr. Walsh says. "We always win. Do you understand?"
"Yes, Dad," says Ryan. "I understand. Our family
always wins."
His father says, "I want you to go faster than last year,
okay? You *will* win today. Okay?"
Ryan is worried but he says, "Yes, Dad."

Tyler, Ryan, and the other riders go to the starting line.
Ryan is worried about the race. He looks at his father.
His father really wants Ryan to win. Ryan looks at Tyler.
He knows Tyler wants to win, too.
"I'll win today. I'm Ryan Walsh! I always win," Ryan thinks.
"I have a good bike and I'm a good rider. I'm very good,"
he thinks.

Tyler looks at Ryan's new bike. "Is that a new bike, Ryan?" he asks.

"Yes," Ryan says. "Do you like it?"

Tyler says, "You have a good bike, but I'm going to win. Let's have a good race."

"Yeah," Ryan replies. "I'll see you at the finish line."

Tyler and Ryan start very fast. They are winning.
They are faster than the other riders. They go faster
and faster. Tyler and Ryan race around a corner.
"Good, I'm winning," thinks Tyler.
Ryan is second but he is going fast, too.

They go up and down. They go through the trees.
They go through a river. It is a very good race.
Tyler is going fast and Ryan is going fast, too.
Now Ryan is winning. And Tyler is second.

They race through some more trees. Tyler and Ryan are tired, but they both want to win today. "I always win!" thinks Ryan. "I can't be second! I won't be second!"
"I'll win today!" thinks Tyler.
They go faster and faster. It is a great race.

They see a gate. They race to it. The first person to the gate will win the race. The two bikes are very close. Ryan goes faster, but Tyler is winning.

"I want to be first to the gate," thinks Ryan. "I want to win! I always win!"

Tyler is winning, but Ryan wants to get to the gate first. He goes faster than Tyler.
Ryan thinks about his father's words. "We always win!" he remembers. "We always win!"
Tyler sees Ryan's bike getting closer and closer.

Ryan does not want Tyler to win. Ryan pushes Tyler.
Tyler shouts, "Hey! What are you doing?"
Tyler's bike hits the gate. He falls off his bike. Ryan goes
through the gate. Ryan goes on to the finish line. He wins
the race.

Ryan gets the cup. His father is very happy.
"Good job, Ryan," says his father.
Ryan says nothing. He is not happy.
Tyler looks at Ryan. Ryan looks at Tyler.
"Umm. . . Dad?. . . ," Ryan says. "I want to tell
you something. . ."

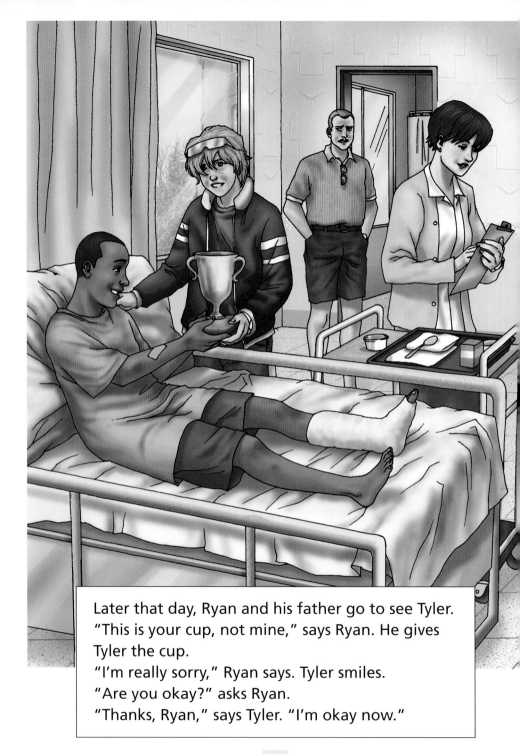

Later that day, Ryan and his father go to see Tyler.
"This is your cup, not mine," says Ryan. He gives
Tyler the cup.
"I'm really sorry," Ryan says. Tyler smiles.
"Are you okay?" asks Ryan.
"Thanks, Ryan," says Tyler. "I'm okay now."